Journeying Back to the World

JOURNEYING BACK
TO THE WORLD

R. K. Meiners

A Breakthrough Book

University of Missouri Press, 1975

University of Missouri Press, Columbia, Missouri 65201
Printed and bound in the United States of America
Library of Congress Catalog Number 74-30339
All rights reserved   ISBN 0-8262-0173-3
Copyright © 1975 by R. K. Meiners

"Miss Business" is reprinted by permission of *Cottonwood Review;* "Mountain Music at Sunset" is reprinted by permission of *Barataria Review;* "My Daughter, Sleeping" and "Bestiary" are reprinted by permission of *Missouri Alumnus;* "Eikampf wears strange disguises" and "Eikampf broods on death" are reprinted by permission of *Red Cedar Review;* "For Hieronymus Bosch" and "Groceries" are reprinted by permission of *The Poetry Bag.* "Two Innocent Pleasures" and "Letter from a Dream" first appeared in *Centennial Review;* "In an excess of beatitude, he claims the fellowship of ants" first appeared in *Happiness Holding Tank.*

Library of Congress Cataloging in Publication Data

Meiners, R K
    Journeying back to the world: poems.

    (A Breakthrough book)
    I. Title.
PS3563.E347J6   811'.5'4   74-30339
ISBN 0-8262-0173-3

For Lynn and Katie and Sally

Contents

Journeying Back to the World

Journeying Back to the World

It is only the fabulous recluses,
only the fabulous voyagers,
who in the end get caught up by their dream
and walk out of time into the wilderness
or sail right off the edge of history.
They leave by different ways;
some go by accident, some by design,
some mighty in their warrior's pride
some wrapping their ordinariness about them
like an old overcoat and slipping into the night:
never knowing when their vessel will founder,
whether the sun will beat with tropic fierceness
on their small thatched roof
or the beneficent southwest wind
bring mild air and warm rain.
Gawain, Ulysses, Ishmael, the Mariner,
these and the others, back of the poles,
searching their fate at land's end,
seeking the questionless answer;
or huddled in the desert like Stylites,
like Elijah with God and the ravens,
waiting for signs and the world's change
for its rage to ripen toward madness.

With the rest of us it is usually different.
We read Thoreau, go to the sea shore,
climb through the brush, identify flowers,
seek wisdom in every shell and sunset,
take long walks through the country,
return, try to recall what we've seen there;
remember the lives of our grandfathers,
think good thoughts of the landscape,
and wonder just what we are doing.

And now I sit in this cabin,
thinking it is time for a voyage,
thinking to head out to the woods,
perhaps to make the true venture
to find the unicorn, the prize.

How often I have moved out,
hid myself from friends and family,
sat and brooded, walked back in my mind
until I found the place that wanted to be alone,
sat there, hoped to be one of those recluses
who would rise, thinking to walk back
to roofs, and children, and society,
only to find all altered, all changed:
to see new sunlight and new colors
playing over the old grooves and surfaces.

But transformation is never that easy.
It is only the fabulous voyager
who has travelled west with the light,
or the recluse possessed by the dream
and compelled by the weight of his story,
bearing his fate like a new name,
who returns with news for the earth,
hoping that someone will listen.

I. Mountains

Mary's Mountain

(for Lee Johnson)

Walking back home
through ponderosa forest

walking down the hill
heading toward home

my pack is crammed
with pine knots wrenched

from decaying tree trunks
that litter the landscape:

as I head toward home
my mind is filled

with thoughts for the dying
and a feel for decay.

This has been a day
for the joys of the dying

a day when I woke
choking on my mortality

and filled the canteen
and gathered my pack

and went with the dog
to climb Mary's mountain:

scrambled over dead pine trunks
scuffled through rotting pine needles

kicking my way
through decaying granite

up to the top
to catch the first light

as it falls on the rocks
where Mary's ashes lie.

Sitting at the top
against a crumbling boulder

and my body is blending
with dead trees and old granite

all of these lovely forms
all of them dying

everything is dying
all forms lose their outlines.

Then the first light fell
on the rocks where she lies

on the rocks where she sat
as a young girl who'd climbed

up from the valley
to catch the first light

and thought of those who'd climbed
the hill long before her

and I laughed at myself
and all of my turmoil:

and thought of the light
as it played through the boulders

thought of the others
who had praised light and rock:

these textures and outlines
took beauty from others

who had sat here before me
loving these forms.

bearing testimony to the hidden lives of men
and their deep connections with things;
and to the hallowed deeds and suffering of the light
as it plays in colors and surfaces,
filling the mind and calling it to rejoice
in its essential and high ancestry.

I pull back from my paper
half in amusement, half in dismay.
I, who have lived so long like a spy
in my language and poems,
with careful guile creeping from figure to figure,
am here discovered gyrating like
some pinchbeck prophet ecstatic
at discovering a spring of consciousness
under every rock and leaf!

No. Not quite that spring.
But in the clear outlines of things
the mind finds itself as though called from its dream,
and with the light weaving on and through surfaces
it finds the fabrics and rhythms of its being.
And even in the greeting of a twisted pine
at three in the morning
under a mountain moon
there is ceremony potent enough
to lead one out of the rituals
and convolutions of estrangement.

Burning Rotten Wood

For five hours I have sat by this stubborn fire
that will neither die nor blaze,
shoving pieces of dry aspen and pine
under the smoldering punky mass
of the rotten log with which I started.
In the presence of other fire it flames up
with vigorous and sham bravado
only to settle into smoky and sputtering sullenness
when the other piece burns out.

It has been a long night,
sitting with notebook open,
and surrounded by other men's books;
the tempting analogy rises
of my inert and sullen mind
creeping along in its amoebic self-consciousness.

Still, should one despise
that pulpy and supine lump
so jealously hugging its fibers to itself
or admire its persistence in its identity?

As they say:
there is motion and abstention from motion.

Notes for an Album History of Buffalo Creek, Colorado

*(In response to a request that I contribute
anything I know or have discovered about
my house & this strange community)*

A hundred years ago the last Ute Indian
left the permanent bivouac on the Creek.
In 1879 they put the railroad through
& named it the Denver, South Park, & Pacific
(it got as far as Leadville).
Ore & lumber came pouring out of the mountains.
Then they sent fashionable young men
as emissaries from the city
(a few years later)
who built houses of Tudor yearnings
& wrote to the *Denver Post*
"our main occupations
are lying & drinking,
& shooting bear & Indians."
But the only two Indians around
lived in a ratty shack
across from the South Platte Hotel
where they were pointed out to day-excursionists.
In the accessible hills they built saw mills
& by 1900 the last ponderosa pine
within convenient reach had been cut
to satisfy the consummate needs
for shingles & siding in Denver & points east.
Ten saw mills & five saloons flourished
until the trees gave out.
The range was open
"from Pike's Peak to Mount Evans"
but the bodies of cattle
had to be fished from the ravines
after every flash flood.

Making the best of that
they decided to build a lake
(lakes are always useful if
you can't stand running water,
or if it is running inconveniently).
They cut ice from it in the winter
& stored it carefully in sawdust.
By 1920 the ice works died.
(Ice saws appeared periodically in auctions.
Still do: authentic bits of nostalgia.)
Pine trees were planted,
lumber cabins reclaimed & occupied.
In the summers they sent up
gentle boys & girls from Topeka & Wichita
who held levee & made month-long
picnics on the slopes.
The cabins were too small
so they brought lumber from Denver
to build larger ones.
The train stopped running.
The ice cream parlor closed.

No minerals have been discovered
in useful amounts (except for
commercially marginal quartz deposits).
The snows are too irregular for skiers.
The land is inhospitable to development
being porous granite & arid,
with water rights tied up
in ancient exclusive contracts.
The South Platte River
furnishes an unpredictable aqueduct for Denver
(elsewhere it is neatly channeled & tunneled).
The South Platte Development Project
has been planned for fifty years,
& last year Spiro Agnew came out

to touch a button that blew the charge
that set another dam in place.
The Denver Water Board
is still poised & eager
to install their major dam
& regularize all of Nature's inconvenience.
("More recreation for more people."
"They might as well flood it,
the hippies have ruined it anyway."
"We can't stop them from moving in,
so we'd better plan for them."
voices in the crowd.)
O Denver, gateway to the West,
Queen City of the Rockies,
perched like a massive spider
in your ever-widening web:
grow more bluegrass lawns,
& install more flush toilets
& more swimming pools
for more people.

At night the stars still gleam—
useless & preternaturally bright.
A bear occasionally raids the trash.
At the last full moon a coyote
made such an unseemly clamor
that everyone's watchdog rushed into the night.

Dear Committee: you asked me
to set down whatever came to mind.
But I don't know who built my house
& I don't know what else might be relevant
to our mutual histories.

Mountain Interlude

Last night,
lacking an ice cube for my drink,
I stuck a frozen trout in the bourbon.
God help me and God help the trout.
The whiskey will look out for itself.

Working at Night in a Mountain Cabin

My child, how am I to work
with you squealing spectral noises
through the walls of the bedroom?
There are only four rooms, and each
is occupied by us, or cats, or dogs.
You moan, a cat stalks in and out,
the dog coughs and rattles her collar.
We dwell on top of each other.
Unless I am to move outside
by night as well as day
it is plain there must be accommodation.
So if you could speak more clearly in your sleep,
and could I have ears to tally your report
with what the wind is doing in the pines,
or some occulted power return
to show me how to climb the hill
and read in the light of moon and stars
the secrets of our voices, eyes, and hands
to bring back in here before the fire
and to my notebooks:
why, then we'd be in business.

Two Innocent Pleasures

Few things so mindless and innocent
can carry the soul farther
than watching a fire grow
from a point of light to a blaze,
watching the heat leap back and forth
between the reflecting surfaces
like a mind dazzled in the earth's polarities:
unless it be to sit at the top of a hill
on the edge of a wide valley
under a high mountain sky
with a red bandanna spread over
the knee, watching the female
hummingbirds probing to make sure
some gigantic crimson blossom
has not flowered anew on the mountainside.
I wish that I could break into flower or flame.

Sunflower

Since June I have been watching
the one lone sunflower growing
on the rotten granite of my hillside.
It has been working upwards all through
the waking dream of high summer,
and each day I have thanked it for itself
and for that glorious poem by Blake.
Common flower and radiant image,
lovely for itself and the light it follows.
And yet there is more.

First come the twinned seed leaves,
fat, ovoid, undefined;
then the next paired leaves
polarizing the stem's axis at right angles;
then the expanding upward spiral commences.
The leaves outline themselves,
lightly toothed, cordate,
lengthened mid-rib, lateral veins,
increased distance between leaves,
five leaves repeated before the angle
with the stem is duplicated.
Then, tightening, the spaces decrease;
the spiral shortens, leaves closer together,
pulling into the close wheel of the calyx.
Now, in late August,
the short season draws to its close.
I stand on the uphill side of the plant
(now more than six feet tall)
staring at the compact geometry,
the corolla struggling to expand itself
into definition under the waning sun;
within that expansion, an enclosing,
as the seedhead pulls the light and heat

into the sheltering, capsuled body:
heat to burn at the center,
heat through the watchful winter.

If it were not urgent
one would shun the pleasures of sentiment:
and take no joy as the seed head forms,
and feel no pain at the casual gaps,
and not feel the chronic incompletenesses,
were the world devoid of ourselves.

If it were not urgent
one might resist the enticements of allegory
and sit in cold comfort savoring the chill air
as one waited in the autumn evening.

Sitting here in the shortening light,
watching the sunflower slowly
erect itself in the twilight
as the sun sinks below Redskin Mountain,
I sit on my porch and wait
for the procession across the South:
Scorpio, red Antares in his belly,
the Archer hastening through Autumn.

Trying to summon my will
out of the wide vortices of summer.
Contracting. Banking the fires for winter.
Waiting for new birth of the light.

II. A Sequence of Late Summers

A Sequence of Late Summers

Fair seed-time had my soul, and I grew up
Foster'd alike by beauty and by fear

1.

As I look back upon my seed-time
I'd like to say that I knew the feel
of deep Illinois loam,
and sank my feet in its mud and dust
and pulled in strength like any ignorant weed.
Or that I heard the tree frogs
calling through the rich summer nights;
that the sound flowing out of the cornfields
gave me tones and rhythms
I'm just beginning to figure out.

And, in a way, all that's true.
But I was dense, thick-headed as a box elder,
and usually ill, hauling my asthma
around like an overripe melon,
wondering why much of the world made me sick
as I gasped my way through the ragweed of August.
It wasn't the world's fault
that I saw so little of its shapes and textures;
but what I'm trying to find out now is
was it mine?

2.

Scene: Wednesday nights. Deep Illinois summer.
The stores stayed open, and just beyond their light,
the corn kept on growing,
reaching through the dog-days' night.
The weedy square beside the Central House,
set with chairs for the weekly festival of the arts.
I played clarinet—

partly for duty, partly in pride,
and partly out of some daft idea
that blowing through that damned reed
would help my lungs.
(O therapeutic muse draw nigh,
breathe on me before I breathe on you.)
We shrilled our ersatz Sousa
until the stores closed and the popcorn gave out.
There I stood, Buster Brown come to the band concert,
Play Orpheus, praying for rain,
shoulders round in red resplendent suit,
wheezing through my clarinet.
The patent leather Sam Browne belt
cut me behind the ear every time
I pulled my neck in to attack high D.

After that, back to my father's store
for a hit of ephedrine,
taking time to steal three packs of cigarettes
(this was 1945), which I peddled
for three bucks and a pack of rubbers in the pool hall.
I carried those around until I lost them,
God knows how long later,
waiting for sweet opportunity to sweep me off my feet
and drown my wheezes in orgasmic delights.
But you know how that goes.
Or that's how it went when I was thirteen in Illinois.

3.

Scene: the Forreston Grove Presbyterian Church,
surrounded by graveyard. It burned down
twenty years ago, to be replaced by some amorphous
brick pile that mocks the graves lying all around.
I have climbed into the belfry of that
old white clapboard-sided church,
and looked down on all those graves

making their silent faithful gestures
toward the church, which tries
to reach high enough to pull all of them to God.
I look toward the rear of the graveyard,
toward the fields of oats and alfalfa
that edge the sides.
Below, a fifteen-year-old boy lies
in my body, behind a tombstone,
holding a .22 rifle. And then
I am lying in that August sun,
rubbing the sweat out of my eyes,
peering around the stone,
waiting for a gopher to show his head.

I can't remember feeling odd
about my part in this tableau;
I was carried away by—well, not blood lust,
but pure desire, a hankering after potency.
So there we were, me behind my grave marker,
the gopher in his hole behind another,
both of us poised six feet above
the bones of my ancestors.
(I don't doubt that he made
forays down to whisper to them,
scratching through their remains
on rodent feet. I'd like to think
that's why I had to kill him:
I couldn't tolerate arrogance
in a votive rodent.
But if that was why, I didn't know it.)
So now I look down through the years
on that round-shouldered fifteen-year-old
poking a rifle around the corner of a tombstone,
and I want to shout: why are you doing that?
Stop. There are better things.
Look at the corn swelling into ears,

trace the letters of your name on the stone,
breathe, and feel the grass give back your breath,
learn the movement of plants,
in God's name wake up,
make provisions for your children.

I hear the summer winds
gathering in the Dakota prairies,
strengthening over the Mississippi,
blowing through the fields of tasseling corn,
and through that burnt-out steeple.

4.

Scene: My uncle's farm. August. I was sixteen.
The shocks of oats stretched out
under the hot Illinois sun,
ten bundles drying in each shock,
under the cap bundle that shed the rain.
In one corner of the north field
they'd brought in a crazy Dutchman
who regularly built fourteen-bundle shocks,
huge mis-shapen things: ass busters,
according to my cousin.
I got so I could get a fifteen-foot load on a hayrack,
all the time praying it wouldn't collapse,
listening to my cousin's laughter
at the town kid's efforts.

Flip off the cap bundle, take two
of the outside ones on the fork,
toss them up so they'd fall
precisely into their place.
With the last four bundles field mice scattered
from where they'd bivouacked.
Every now and then I'd nail one
with a tine of my fork, and feel sick.
Strange. I would go to any length

to do a gopher or rabbit or squirrel to death
by design, and get sick
at killing a mouse by accident.

Back in the barnyard we'd line our hayracks up,
one on each side of the thresher;
we'd work so fast hurling bundles into the feeder
my uncle would scream like a demented scarecrow
from his work in the growing straw pile
—do you fools want to break the thing down?
Exactly. Occasionally we would succeed,
and while wiser ones repaired,
we'd sneak behind the granary with a half-a-dozen
bottles of Schlitz we'd swiped from the ice-tub
and drink ourselves silly,
talking of baseball and women.
He was nineteen. I sixteen.

When I was seventeen he pitched baseball
against my team and struck me out three times,
laughing like a fool. The fourth time
I hit an outside curve off his left knee
and yelled from first base
—a foot higher and all your kids
will be someone else's.

Three days later he was dead.
Bulbar polio, they said.
I was in some coma of my own
and never saw him buried,
waking days later to hear that he was dead,
retiring back into my sleep.
People whispered around me for weeks
like shocks of oats leaning together
and said, why did the other one die,
as I wheezed on toward recovery.

Tell me Jim, tell me cousin,
do they build better loads of bundles in heaven?
They build them nowhere else.
All the threshing machines are gone.
The oats still yellow in the August sun,
but the granary is gone: the barn, the house.
Great combines stalk like dinosaurs
through the phosphated fields of our homeland,
the lushest farm land of the continent.
Nobody swears at the Dutchman's heavy shocks,
no mice run in terror from the forks.
And unless some Disney comes along
and forms the upper midwest carnival of nostalgia
no one will ever load another bundle of oats.
That's another skill gone its way, my cousin,
that's gone like you into the grave.

5.

Scene: August, 1970. South Fork of the South Platte.
Six miles above Deckers, three below Cheeseman Dam.
We'd hiked in by the Gill Trail, above the river,
glistening below like a corridor
winding through the eternal heart of August.
Four of us: Lynn, me, Katie and Sally,
edging our way over the rotten granite
at the outer edge of summer.
And one other: a poodle who looked like a sheepdog
and imitated mountain goats: leaping
from the highest rocks she could find,
making us long for animal legs or wings.
Working our way down to the river,
I went first to stop falling bodies,
for both kids threatened to go arse over teacup
down the talus to the river, a hundred feet below.
Down in the canyon, we worked along the river's edge
until the boulders got too steep
to crawl over or around.

Lynn looked around and said
—the cliffs look like Hokusai drew them.
Decided she'd draw the river anyway,
with the house-sized boulder where
the current moved back on itself
and under the rock ledge,
emerging in five linked but separate tongues
around the smaller rocks below.
I sprawled against the pack
while the kids scrabbled among the rocks
until Katie found a fly amanita, beautiful and deadly.
Then the dog discovered a column of ants,
barked at them in idiot delight,
and summoned me to action.
I hauled the rod out of the pack,
fitted the four sections together,
started to work my way through the boulders.
A quarter of a mile along the canyon
I took two browns out a deep pool
formed by a fallen Engelmann spruce
lying across the stream;
twitched the fly from their jaws,
watched them flicker back into the current.

Sitting on the bole of the fallen spruce
I stared at the clouds floating past Long Scraggy
where it curls around the river
like Fafnir guarding his treasure.
August gathered itself around me.
In an immense silence, the very river stilled;
it narrowed and flattened, and cut between rounded hills
below the White Oak bridge;
and underneath the Colorado sun
the Illinois prairie spread out.
A twelve-year-old boy shuffled along Elkhorn Creek,
throwing rocks at the fat carp that nosed the bottom,
fins barely moving against the lazy current.

It was no dream. I could hear the jays
calling from the stand of spruce;
cicadas whined, and I stared at the rocks
showing above the dancing water,
and I moved from August to August through my life.
Late summer flowered.
August spread out like a glowing field
within the light that held my eyes,
and the light that was my eyes.
The sun shone through the trees and on the water,
and the boy looks down the river
at what he is to become;
memory joggles memory, and the late summer flowers
dot the fence rows around the grain fields
in a continual emblem of summer.
Through the August sun I hear my children
shouting downstream, shouting down my years,
calling me to come,
to look at the flowers they've discovered,
growing through the summers of our life.

III. Music and Children

Gravedweller's Song

There's a hole in my roof.
Is someone excavating?
Is someone digging for me?
Here I lie,
wound in my life.
I'm wrapped like Tut the Egyptian,
wound round with dust and stupor.

Someone's scratching my face.
There's nothing there.
My brain has already vanished.
It's been hooked through my nostrils,
pulled out with a wire
to save my soul.

Now it is drying.
It is walnut sized.
It will be cracked and ground,
sprinkled like condiments and spices,
decorating the palates of gourmands.

Let it go.
Why should I need it, lying here?
I am surrounded by bitter essences,
the oils of astringency.
I am shrinking.
I am already small and hard.
My skin cracks.

I am waiting to see
if a fabulous butterfly
springs from my mouth.

Playing Fiddle Music on the Banjo

I live for weeks at a time
obsessed by the old melodies,
weaving in and out
of the infinite subtleties of their movement.
I play them over and over again
like a man possessed
by some lunatic daemon—
partly in sheer delight,
partly offering homage to the dead.

One night, after ten minutes
of playing the Gildleroy Hornpipe together,
tossing its phrases back and forth
in an antique, private colloquy,
the fiddler stopped, shook his head,
and said
—that is the damnedest *snaky* tune,
it goes round and round
and keeps coming back to the beginning.

So every time I play the thing now,
fingers winding over the fretboard,
mind winding through metaphysics,
I ask myself at the same time
what the hell I think I'm doing,
an aging minstrel with no audience
wrestling with this insane instrument
with its fifth string fixed like a horizon
reminding me of my finitude,
chiming the hour of death,
and that persistent daemon whispers:
with only a little more grace,
some fluidity and purity of will,
you might even be making images,
images of time and eternity,
going round and round like the sacred serpent
coiling tail to head.

Musicians

How many of my best hours
have been spent with musicians?
Working out a clawhammer passage
or listening to a new bowing,
making new versions of the old tunes
on guitar, banjo, and fiddle:
Soldier's Joy, say, or Fisher's Hornpipe.

Musicians: speaking of and playing
intricate alternatives of each melody;
telling stories of the old ones;
swapping licks, polishing tunes;
usually lying to each other
as if we all had the lyre of Apollo
hidden at home in the back of the attic,
along with a Martin herringbone
or a mint-condition 1915 Gibson F model.

Musicians: their endless talk of instruments.
Sometimes after a session
it has run through my mind
so much that in my dreams
I have seen ladders of banjos and fiddles
ascending and descending like angels of God
singing of the divine hierarchies.

Musicians: sometimes, strings vibrating
under my fingers I have thought
we might all be Pythagoreans
joined in the mysteries,
celebrants of Orpheus,
our very bodies our own
best musical instruments,
and I have said yes,
the very lyre of Apollo

weaving in and out of the endless harmony,
and thought of some supreme old fiddler
bowing to himself in secret accord
with the melody he was shortly to join,
Uncle Charlie Higgins, playing Blackberry Blossom
over and over in his 90th year
because he *knew*.

Musicians: leaning back between tunes,
emptied of that by which they were possessed,
falling heavily into speech,
sucking deeply at cigarettes,
dropping them into empty beer cans:
hands moving nervously
over fretboards, around pegheads,
like pairs of caged rodents.

Musicians: emptied, hollow
as the empty fifths of mountain harmony,
the "high lonesome sound";
soul wandering through sound
like some lonesome ghost,
music going away, music returning,
breathing in, breathing out.

Musicians: how sad they are when silent.
Sometimes I wish that I could play forever.

Mountain music at sunset

I stood and watched Bill Monroe
and heard the high austere perfection of his voice
and thought of the old players and singers,
and of the depleted land,
and of the burnt-out jokes of the Grand Ole Opry.

His fingers chased over the Gibson mandolin
as he leaned toward his banjo player,
a kid from Boston thirty years younger
who played as though he'd bartered his yankee soul
for seventy years of tradition and infallible hands.

The old and young leaned together:
behind them, the shadows of the elders
seemed to move in concert,
the fiddler bowing from course to fine,
the claw-hammered banjo picking Bill Cheatham.
And something not quite of myself said,
no voice is wholly lost to him who will hear it;
and something not quite other replied,
no music from the soul can leave it traceless,
nor leave the world untouched.

And as they played the music
against the sunset of Bean Blossom, Indiana,
the dance of the fingers on the fretboard
seemed from and of that place;
and the tension in that throat,
the nervous hawklike anger,
flowed out of the very land,
the pillaged streams and mountains.

To Hell with Fiddlers

(to the memory of Fate Norris)

"Of . . . Fate Norris, very little is known. . . . He
was probably a contemporary of Tanner and Puckett, and
is believed dead. On the Skillet Lickers' recordings
he plays banjo, and is usually almost inaudible. On
some of his recordings with Gid and Arthur Tanner his
singing and playing come across much better. He also
used to play a one-man band."
—Liner note on reissue of the Skillet Lickers,
*   an old-time string band that always used two*
*   fiddlers, Gid Tanner and Clayton McMichen, and*
*   often added a third, Lowe Stokes.*

Listening to these old records
I can occasionally hear enough
to know you were not inaudible
from lack of skill or vigour;
and I can hear your banjo
by suppressing some of the highs,
and filtering out some
of those omnivorous fiddles;
but the miracles of electronics
cannot bring you back, Fate Norris.
And so I brood on your name,
as I think you may have:
into which you must have settled heavily,
maybe stretching your limbs
until you filled all parts of it.
I wish I had known you,
to see whether you were really
one of those late-born ones
who drop into life knowing
that nothing was right,
and nothing should be changed.

It's the fiddlers who have always claimed
they had some special access to God,
or when the drink and black humours
were on them they winked and said
it was the devil after all:
and played The Devil's Dream
or said they rode the Devil's hobbyhorse.

But, Fate Norris, you and I know different.
And if they and their fiddles
enchant us out to the very realm
of air and light and pure vowels
where Lucifer breathes the eternal sunlight
we know who brings it all back again,
who makes the music habitable
and gives it a place on earth
where we can live with it,
who places it in the ears
and puts in the sharp staccato
of objects and consonants and domestic stuff.

Fate Norris, I see you sitting there
behind those great lantern-jawed egoists
and you are playing, playing,
and the rhythm of your claw-hammered banjo
brings me back out of my dreams
and into myself, once more charmed
into the sweet oppositions of the music
where the sharp singularity calls forever
and asserts itself against its opposite,
defining the whole.

My Daughter, Sleeping

Now after all these years
I know indeed that there are moments
when the Presence comes through
and tells the endless tale of origins.

The music begins.
The musician bends over his instrument
and, singing, a different face
looks through his eyes.

And there, on the pillow
the face of my child in repose.
I can read there
the confirmation of reality,
word after word.

Now I can see the testimony
that in the depths
all is as it must be
and that all shall be well.
Can anything be disastrous
as my child turns aside into sleep
and, turning outward
into the wide cone of reality,
brings back the news that all is well?

I must change my life.

Miss Business

Grubby hands working constantly:
we called you the furious flycycle
as you churned away, from project to project
like something out of that book by Jan Wahl
(except that you are the wrong sex;
why can't child-inventor-geniuses be girls?).
My daughter, how did your parents
ever bring forth something like you?
Fluttering in your welter of activity,
through how many generations of indolence,
nervous breakdowns, plattdeutsch stubbornness
and black Irish spleen did you have to work
before you'd generated enough karma
to spring running into your life and ours?

Perhaps trailing clouds of glory,
but certainly trailing black eyes,
ink-smeared face, endless bits of paper,
yarn, masking tape, countless desiccated bottles of glue,
you have sprawled through our lives
and leave us wondering what to do for you
and what we have done to ourselves.

Late tonight I sit in this room,
watching my hand hesitate above the paper.
From the shelves across the room
I am watched in turn by the eyes of nineteen owls.
They stare at me out of wood, clay, and stone,
and those that stare most pointedly
are the three fabric and yarn versions
created by you and your sister to compete
with the others in the collection.
And as I hesitate, cursing the words that will not come,
I make my usual tired joke:
no owls for Athena tonight.

O my daughter, at eight years of age,
and without the slightest thought of craft or inspiration,
an endless series of pictures, puzzles,
devices, constructions—assemblages that
would delight the souls of Rube Goldberg
and Yves Tangueley—pour forth from you;
and overhead in his third-floor pigeon loft
your lame-brained father
stares at his hands frozen on the paper.

Last night, overcome by irritability
and my own uncertainty,
unable and unwilling to face one more bit
of exuberance at the day's end,
I shouted at you, and you went to bed crying.
Later I went into your room,
and saw you'd fallen asleep reading *The Last Battle*,
from the Narnia books I'd just finished
reading at bed times.
I wonder, my daughter, whether
you were checking on me,
to see if you could trust me to get the story right;
maybe you were wondering
whether there were angry fathers in Narnia.

Tonight the lion will move through your dreams,
and darker shapes will stalk in the shadows
as I walk off the edge of my sleeping;
and perhaps we may dream ourselves
back beyond our memories
and meet in a landscape of perfect color,
where lovely forms and shapes delight our eyes,
and every new turning of the path
will be peopled with the marvelous
beasts and gargoyles of your imagining.

My Daughter's Pictures

First sticks, and sticks crossing sticks,
and then loops, and circles in the sticks,
then crooked sticks and circles stuck together,
trying to be animals, trying to struggle upright.
Now animals are coming:
            cats, horses, birds, birds, birds,
            and horses with wings
silly gross horses with wings
            you who never heard of Pegasus,
            and where did you see a horse?

Here's a mother flying horse
and the baby horse, with wings, but tight closed eyes,
and a baby dog with no eyes.
And now the people come,
and the people have no eyes and no wings,
sad people, pinching their arms against their ribs

            people who cannot fly
            people with crossed-out faces

            (darling, what are you saying?
            how will you suffer this world?)

More horses are coming,
and serpents with teeth,
and more animals
all manner of animals with wings.

And finally the sun.
The animals fly around the sun,
the animals fly all over the sky,
and they fly through the grass
            which is around the sun,
the animals fly, and they are singing,
singing that that the sun is shining,

that the grass is glorious,
that the trees are happy with the animals.

And now the people are smiling,
they smile for the first time,
now that they have eyes,
now that they hold out their arms.

They are carrying sticks,
they are building with sticks,
they are building a pickety fence,
they are building a stairway to heaven

the birds are flying with the animals,
and they are singing that heaven
        is peopled with ourselves,
and even serpents can smile,
and pain can smile through its teeth.

IV. Memory, Nightmares, Dreams

Groceries

In the cinnamon and dust of my father's store
I worked, a mulish slave to order,
sweating and hauling in the basement,
spreading confusion like spices
through all those dank pasteboard corridors,
my father's provisions for the town.

"Think fast," I cried, hurling a Campbell's can,
"or another mouse goes to meet the mousemaker."

One day I broke the lift three times
offering it too many cases.
In honor of the occasion I promoted it;
it became a dumb waiter, its wounds, ruptures;
its handle swung limply.
My father, waiting for groceries,
stomped overhead.

On Saturdays I emerged into the fresh,
sabbatical air to candle eggs.
I handled them portentously, holding them
carefully to the light which shone
through the hole in the Karo can,
and wondered what to look for.

I could lift three dozen eggs at once,
never breaking one (except those in which
I decreed a flaw; they flew
to their election against the wall
of the Ford Garage across the alley).

I left to find my life, to escape
the charm of those crates, to seek
the life of the egg, the mouse.

     Row on row
the crates stretch out with their magic wares:
box after box, corners split, spilling
canned milk here, chopped meat there,
hoisted from the dusty basement.

Vortices

When I was a young boy
still full of the aftertow of eternity
and in love with its movements and images
I used to sit and will the world
into fragments that spun down
the vortices of time, bright tunnels
leading backward, forward without end.

Eternity.
I would close my eyes
and look down through those whirling
funnels and breathe to myself,
"forever," "never an end,"
until my imagination collapsed
in a pleasant vertigo
reeling in from the peripheries
of time and space.
It was my private cosmic recreation
available any time I found myself alone
at ease and confident in my powers.

One chilly Saturday morning,
standing in some childish spite
before the marble bricks
of my grandparents' hearth
(in the front room used only on Sundays
where I used to creep to hug
my secret knowledge to myself),
I watched my pinched face
reflected back in the shining
mineralized prisms of the fireplace
and murmured to myself
"I wish they'd die, I wish they'd all die."
And terror came flashing back
on me as swiftly as if those bricks

had opened before my eyes
and some astral wind of unbearable
cold and brightness
had swept me out beyond the stars.

I grasped the mantel and rubbed
my forehead on the greens and bronzes
of the marble, but nothing
in that room or around it
bore any look of comfort
for a young boy dizzied by mortality.

After Summer

All summer
I have been sitting in the sun and reading,
sitting before the firelight putting words on paper.
I have been surrounded by birds and animals,
birds and animals have haunted my language:
they have been flying all through the summer light,
they scuttle through the dark outside the door.
In the slanting light of fall they are restless
and I am surfeited with light and language.

Enough.
I am closing the books and will read no more.
I am putting away my pencils and paper.
Lord of lights,
Lord of the eyes that receive them,
care for the birds and the animals,
be with me as I sink wordless into autumn.

Selasphorus platycercus, selasphorus rufus

Hummingbirds. Our words catch
    but the sound of their going.
In our drab way we call them
    Broadtail and Rufous.
Someone with eyes for the light
    called them *selasphorus,*
the flamebearers. They dive
    through the mountains all summer:
messengers from another life,
    lacing our memories with the sun.

In the midst
    of this gray inland winter
it is hard to remember
    the flash of colors.
But the earth is cloaked
    in a mantle of light,
and the Fire still burns
    at the depths of December
waiting to leap
    into the winter cold, winter dark.

Sunlight and Memory

(for Owen Barfield)

1.

Before the long mirror
on the sunny wall of the south room
I would arrange myself
and stare at my eyes staring back
out of their freckled recesses.
Then close them:
carefully turn, gather my body
into desirable postures,
postures of grace and swiftness:
eyes open, and whirl
to see the back of my head
still caught in the glass
as if by sheer quickness
I could leap into transcendence
and look back through the eyes
of Berkeley's divine observer.

2.

Sitting against this tree,
feet propped on granite boulder,
staring at lichen patterns,
at the sun flashing from the water
falling through Spring Gulch
I slowly turn on my childhood:
as if by staring at lichen
I could summon out of the rock
those eyes and that freckled face,
could whirl on the glass of memory
and catch there some calm,
some sweet knowledge,
that flees from me as fast
as I try to recall it.

3.

They call it nostalgia,
the collectors of experience,
and they turn blindly
never knowing where the return leads,
stumbling against the faces
that clutch like thorns in the path
the past throws up to their eyes;
or hear in the shadowy distance
the fabled horns of paradise
sounding thinly along
the broken waters of memory:
never knowing how they got there,
why they return or where,
why the pain keeps recurring
on the road that turns home.

4.

Staring at lichen and
the sun seems to flicker
and tracings of shade and
light cling to the rock.
Is it light that touches
around the dark crevices?
or lichen's gray-green fingers
teasing the eye into
the red freckled granite?
Old scenes leap, as they do,
to the mind, to the eye:
mind slows, stops, hovers
among the old pictures
and eye traces where it leads
and hand hovers and
the mind leaps toward itself
like sunlight returning to water.

The patterns of lichen on rock
are like words I wrote
long ago in my sleep
from which I slowly awaken
to the sound of falling water
flowing into that mirror
where the boy whirls around
and catches the eyes looking back.
Boy's eyes, older than lichen,
older than rock, flowing like water
under the dazzling sunlight,
called from the ancient sunlight.

Bestiary

It seems that for months each night
I've heard those persistent beasts
scuffling through the coathangers,
pawing the shoes, snuffling
in the pockets for mothballs,
clawing though my clothes for scents.
What do they wish?
What nourishment can they find
in discarded paisleys and foulards?
Why should their sharp teeth
worry my fabrics and textures?

Come now, go to the closet door
and lay it open.
All its enticing wares
sprawl in the moonlight.
Perhaps there, murmuring
a throaty tune in the night,
curled among my vests will be a beast.

He will say: fly the profane world,
full of light as a chameleon.
Seek with me the warmth,
the pleasant shadow behind these shirts!
If you attend, a truth lurks in that cuff;
and there, behind your coats,
a gleam so true you dare not leave it.

Follow it with me through this wall.

Letter from a Dream

I have been coming to the post office
every night for years,
looking for my mail box,
searching for a message,
a letter telling me to come home,
that everyone is waiting to see me.

I know something about dreams:
I know this is preparation, and ritual.
It is vital to take part,
and never miss a night.
I walk through the front door,
through the echoing hall and down stairs.
The mail room is down below, waiting;
the mystery may be hiding there still,
mummified in its mailbox
like some sacred corpse waiting for spring.

No one ever speaks.
Usually it is empty
(except for one who gives a sidelong glance
as we pass each other on the stair
as if he, too, were looking).
He leaves a wordless question hanging:
—have you come to find your hidden life?
the one that must be here one day?
Will there be some miniature angel,
poised, a tiny messenger,
waiting for you to announce yourself?

And then comes the worst part, when I think,
maybe I *did* find it once,
looking like a crumpled postcard
to be thrown out like any other
third-class junk, and now I shall
never see my secret name.

One night my vision cleared.
I saw the secret hidden
in the last row next to the wall,
close to the floor.
Kneeling down I whispered through the empty vaults:
I am here. I have come.
Proclaim yourselves. What do you hold?
I waited for any tremor of response,
and waited.
Nothing moved. Nothing spoke.
And I knew then that if there had been even one murmur
I'd have seized it by its throat to make it yield,
as in the days when I was
the fastest sneak thief in the upper midwest,
opening locks faster than the postal service
        could change them,
not so much in malice as in sheer loneliness
        and vacancy.

In the name of heaven
what am I searching for?
Why keep coming down here?
Why keep participating, when all it yields
is a grubby post-mistress
muttering stories about me,
thumbing through my past like she belonged there,
sending through demands for payment?

No one has the answers to these questions.
At least no one has told me.
Like everyone I long ago read in Freud,
but he, said poor Henry Bones
(for whom I nightly pray),
was some or mostly all wrong about dreams.
Occasionally an old gentlemen leans kindly
        into my life
as I enter that front door

and, wearing such learning that it frightens me,
he tells me to persevere.

Night after night I find myself on the stairs
hoping that nothing out of other dreams
hides in the shadows.
One night a door may fall open and,
peering through, my sight will
fall on roses, and hills of flowers
    drenched in sunlight,
and wind blowing in from some far field,
through gardens more fertile than those
that brighten all the seed catalogs of the world.

For Hieronymus Bosch

I was lying in bed eyeing a folio
with hell and heaven on glossy Swiss plates.
Blue Flemish light spread from book to window,
and my eye and bed began to dilate.
The air grew thin and chill with the fall
of shadows; outside my narrow door
in the breathing darkness of the hall
things moved quickly through the corridor.
My room now seemed to be a cell
and I sat numbly, not daring to stir:
I had dreamed some exotic hell.
Someone blew incense through the air.
I was choking. I turned around,
gobbling like a guppy in my fright,
and saw the serpent, precisely wound
beside my chair, half hidden in the night.
He bowed, and on the floor traced white shapes:
trefoils, arabesques, that seemed to melt
and dance into forms like men or apes
who shuffled gaily with my father's pelt
obscenely dangling around their ears
like old moss stuck on toads as hair.
I breathed, and said, "but these fears
are merely mine, old jokes and private despair
circling like Bosch's blackbirds around a hill
crowded with old carrion."

       So I took my pen
and scrabbled for paper to graph these ills:
surely I could tame and record this specimen
for later, quiet thought?

       I raised my head
and the serpent nodded, turned and bowed,
went under my chair, emerged beside the bed,

growing hands and claws, wearing a mortarboard,
bearing a diploma which certified
Blank a man of learning and courtesy.
"Will the candidate step forward?" he sighed,
fixing a dark, friendly eye on me.

I groped through memory to find some prayer
for driving devils and nightmares from the room.
But he smiled, gave me a quizzical stare
and waved the diploma, pointed at a loom
that stood at the bed's end on the floor
with cords like veins, which seemed to be my own
though I swear I had not missed them before.
He bent to his weaving, the fabric spun
all around him, covering bed, loom, wall.

The curtains blew gently out in the hall.

Another Nocturne

Last night I had this disrespectful dream
of Marcel Duchamp strolling
down the leafy avenues of paradise
where he met Spike Jones.
Duchamp smiled and signed
his name on Jones's forehead,
and Jones squeezed Duchamp's nose
and the scores of three Wayne King waltzes
and a Sousa march fell from Duchamp's mouth,
along with a little flag that said "artist."
Then they made their way, arm in arm,
through this heaven of aesthetes,
marching off to put a firecracker
under Wallace Stevens' hammock.
And I am recording this because
just before I woke some voice
from above or below the dream said:
"write it down. Who gave you the right
to decide just what is significant?"

Dreaming of Poetry

Hovering above the body in my bed
I return from journeys
through the dictionaries of the night
and settle heavily into the fibres and nerves.
Feeling the burgeoning syntax of consciousness
the body stretches toward the light.
I lie in bed, dreaming of unfinished poems,
of words lying in folded heaps,
and ribbons of words, shining with significance,
glistening their way back into the dark
like the tracks of cosmic snails
or the writhing of a lean and stubborn soul
digging in its nails and protesting
its return to the uneasy light of day.

Still half beyond the Threshold
the reluctant soul stretches itself above the bed
and settles down. I dream of poems:
soft and unfinished, curled on themselves,
poems that speak of the vanishing of sensation,
poems of the birth of memory,
images of the drying of the throat
after the last slow drink
from some oasis in a fevered desert
parched of consciousness and spirit.

Still drifting, I ease out of bed and down the stairs.
My dog nods on the steps like a sleepy chrysanthemum.
Coffee, toast: the familiar outlines harden.
The morning paper lies on the table
waiting to wrap the edges of the day around me.
But each day the words are new.
The table has the feel of strangeness,
and the familiar light has the look of strangeness,
and consciousness has the feel of strangeness:

as if it had been recreated in my dreaming,
as if some small tailor had spent all night
sewing new clothes, with old pleats and creases.

So the day moves.

Tonight I will feel fatigue
beckoning me into my body,
and I shall enter, crossing the Threshold.
Sense after sense turns inward
like hounds searching a valid dream.
Drifting into sleep I greet my grandfather
and ask him what I might claim,
what image? A fork, slicing into the loam,
grubbing up hills of potatoes?
Is there an image lying at those roots
to be held against the years?

The room vanishes below my dreams.
The lonesome body is watched, margined,
ordered by objects. Lines are drawn
reaching from my chin to the wardrobe;
cufflinks unused for a decade
exert their silent claims;
old suits crouch sullenly over their hangers,
hungering for my flesh.

Morning. Recrossing the Threshold.
Tidings from the dead.
I am touched with the language of being.
The light falls into my room
and I lie in bed, dreaming of poems.

V. Disguises and Mysteries

Eikampf wears strange disguises

No one there could say what inner need
brought Eikampf to spend his time pacing the hall
or why he'd decked himself in hat and tweed
and peered closely at every door along the wall.

"I am checking patterns of egress,"
says Eikampf, to stifle their dismay
while he secretly searches for a witness
who can testify that he (Eikampf) came *in* the usual way.

Now shifty Eikampf comes down the steps
wearing a cap and pushing a broom.
He looks to the right, looks to the left,
and hurriedly backs into the first room.

Eikampf opens the top drawer of the file:
he will get to the bottom of this game.
Now he reads the "E" folder from the pile.
"Eikampf: there is no one by that name."

To Eikampf's mind conclusions swarm:
if he has vanished, he must be free.
He goes to the desk, takes out a form,
and requisitions a new identity.

Smiling, Eikampf leaves the room,
walks smartly out with bowler and cane;
and one, carrying dustpan, mop, and broom,
says "Good evening. Eikampf is my name."

Eikampf broods on death

Eikampf has conceived the thought
that when man is born he begins to die.
This so unnerves him that he is brought
to wonder on fate, and life, and destiny.

Eikampf takes to inventing puzzles,
arranging words to pass the time,
feeding caramels to dogs wearing muzzles,
inventing perversities, meditating crime.

Eikampf falls into deep despair,
ponders the cruelty of being born,
sees madness floating through the air,
accepts with grace his fate forlorn.

Learned Eikampf deals in wit,
takes pleasure in mocking the sublime,
proclaims the deep beauty of common shit,
finds no paradox too hard to climb.

Late one awful Thursday evening,
God calls in drunken Eikampf's mind;
and worlds on worlds go their own way, spinning
out beyond the stars, leaving him behind.

**Eikampf attends many parties
and dreams he has total recall**

Eikampf, on the authority of the best texts,
has trained himself to distrust words,
yet he lacks adequate escapes and pretexts
when they buzz his ears like swarming birds.

So Eikampf stands against the wall,
trying to hide behind his glass,
while a smiling lady strides down the hall
apparently determined to make a pass.

Wary Eikampf makes his face stern;
says, sorry, he has no light;
commands his feet and hips to turn,
follows his hands as they flutter into flight.

Eikampf closely watches teeth
as they bite the world into hors-d'oeuvre-sized bits,
descries the captive skull beneath
the ambitious cheeks, the eager lips.

Now he finds sweet respite in wine,
he becomes a connoisseur of gins,
an epicure of bourbon, scotch, and rye:
anything that lets him love his sins.

Boorish Eikampf leaves the scene,
staggers toward his perilous bed,
swallows two darvon, one dramamine,
and reads his life from the back of his forehead.

In an excess of beautitude
he claims the fellowship of ants

I love to write these poems
in which events lean against each other
and lave themselves in their importance.
Here is the landscape covered with clouds,
the tips of rocks become visible
and excite the grandiloquence of the eye;
the forms of trees exert themselves,
preening on the satin of consciousness.
Flowers and insects appear here and there:
die, disappear, decay, offering
convenient simulacra of ourselves.
O for a poetry of dust and pebbles,
a muse of sheer orthography!
All these goings and comings!
The very letters dance like ants
delving deep burrows:
there they go,
into their dens of significance.

Lapsus Linguae

Turning the pages
of this tattered notebook
with its half-finished lines,
fragments of language,
and pieces of insight,
I came to this page
with the dried flattened body
of a gold and red spider.
I wonder what words
could be found in my store,
what great intuitions
might persuade the world
it had made a fair exchange?
Sing, heavenly muse.

Winter Song

(for Owen Barfield)

Now comes the longest night
and darkness coils the earth;
the serpent devours all light
but that which waits its birth.

On the first night of thirteen
though cold has hardened the ground
the sun burns deep within:
heat which the winter surrounds.

Then I saw a fair white beast
shining through winter's door
as though the sun had leaped
from the frozen earth's core.

And then I saw him run,
the light caught on his horn,
the bearer of the sun
under the stars of Capricorn.

Three Orphic Songs

"the heavy bear. . ."

First Orphic Song

Down in the cave
with the bears and the bones
I sent my words:
they came back stones.

Stones for the graves,
bones for the head,
but the bear and the words
shall rise from the dead.

Second Orphic Song

Down in the cave
still lie the stones
and memory waits
in the calcified bones;

and the bear mutters
as he turns in his sleep,
the stones watch the earth
where gnomes travel deep;

and the minerals shine
and remember the light:
fossils and memory
guard the long night.

Again the bear murmurs,
through his dream move the words
engraved in the stones
that will waken the birds,

that will call out the light
and bring forth the leaves.
He breathes in his sleep.
The cave also breathes.

Third Orphic Song

Bone Song

Bones cover the hillside,
more bones every night
and all these small deaths
surround the frail light.

Skull bone and scapula,
quick mouse and light bird,
now quickness and lightness
flow back to the word

that first called them forth
from their wait in the soul
that gave them their kind:
dove, squirrel, vole.

> Old bear still slumbers
> asleep in himself
> dreaming his bones
> white caves, full of wealth
>
> shining like silver
> that runs through the dark
> where mineral beings
> speak in the rock
>
> in words lacing his sleep
> with crystalline forms;
> quartz words, and cobalt,
> whisper to his bones.

Above the bear's cave
lie hillsides of small bones.
He dreams of these deaths.
They sing of his own.

VI. Living in the Light

Bird Reflections

I.

In the leafless branches
of my winter hedge

five goldfinches dance
above a black squirrel

waiting for their turn
at seeds and cracked corn

and in all that flurry
there is not one concern

for the waters running darkly
over the floor of my basement

not a moment's thought
for my dark wet places

so why do I feed them
all through the winter

unless it could be
the flash of their movements

the way olive feathers
catch the thin light

and the bills slant backward
to bright black eyes

that watch boughs waiting
for their yellow leaves

II.

The branches of my winter hedge
hold their life close

and five goldfinches weave
bird forms down through time

above the black squirrel
who abandoned their wings

olive feathers and bright beaks
gifts of the sunlight

hollow bones support
a bird made of air

bird flesh is made warm
by feathers of leaves

that dance through the branches
above my cold places

and so I feed them
give gifts to the air

give back some small light
to light that is weaving

through branches that wait
for small thoughts to flit

up from the basement
like feathers of leaves

For the Osculation of the Sun

I think I ought to be honest
about where this title came from.
I got it from Robert Kelly,
but it turns out he isn't responsible.
Turning through his *The Mill of Particulars*
I read the poem to Olson
and the one with the horny old man
descending in skinny desire
on the nubile maiden, both caught
in some strange dialogue between
John Keats and Saint Paul and the joys
of the flesh, frozen in their pleasure
on the clay of a red-figured cup
(and Kelly's right, it's not a performance,
not a test; but Keats is dead;
and the gaunt old lover strains
to enter that timeless flesh):
and thought, well, that's nice,
now what? And I turned,
as one does, to the front, and read
all those fine titles, and found:
"The Occulation of the Sun."

Lord, he can't mean it, I thought,
turning in haste to p. 18
and there it stood:
"The Occultation of the Sun."

Well, hell. Good enough. Occultation.
I've thought of that before.
There are some fine metaphors
and some mighty strange history
clinging to *that* word.
But I was set for osculation,
for a sort of cosmic soul kiss:

the Children of Adam
soaring to the burning center of life!
The scrawny but imperious
middle-aged-poet takes flight
and really gets up to the source of it all,
or gets down on the source,
if that's how it should turn out.

How did I read "osculation"?
The printer did some tricks,
but no amount of chasing through dictionaries
(including my micrographic OED,
Bausch & Lomb lens in hand)
would justify all this extravagance.
So, Robert Kelly, I can't
thank you for the metaphor.
I've only your misprint and my tired eyes
and income-tax-addled brain
and the eternally whimsical muse
to thank for the osculation of the sun.

Oh, Robert Kelly, what shall I do?
You have set my head spinning
around the sun, my head is a sun,
and the whole world comes to kiss it
in an ecstasy of happy accident.
I thank you for the precedent
if not for the metaphor,
for don't tell me you didn't hear
"Mill" playing around in some
legal humdrum about "Bill of Particulars"
and turn the world inside out
to grind in your mill with a dusty miller
grunting out and sweating
over his daily ration of grains and facts.
As you say: "It was the Mill of Particulars
because we heard the word."

And I heard "Osculation."
So Be It.

Or *was* it occulation?
Non occulus sed oculus: mundi oculus.
The sun is the eye of the world.
We are surrounded by eyes,
and by oculated butterflies,
and the insatiable oculation of growing plants:
everywhere eyes, springing from the light.
Oh, Robert Kelly,
have we in our madness given eyes to the sun?
The sun looks down on our folly still
—who are we, Ecclesiasticus?
His eyes are full of light
for poets moiling around in their dark holes
like moles grubbing for worms,
digging ecstasy under chicory roots:
light in the eyes of potatoes under the earth,
light in the eyes of Apollo the far-darter,
light for millers lifting their heavy rations
of wheat and millets and milled fact,
for old men full of dreams of desire,
who yearn after smooth young thighs.
The oculation of the sun.
Have we given him eyes
or has he given ours?
Were the eyes created for the light,
or the light for the eyes?
Robert Kelly, see what you have done!
If you do not watch out
you will have me re-reading Goethe.
Farbenlehre: that's what we need.

Then will the light's life-bestowing kiss
and the poet's life-devouring kiss
not meet in the sweet stasis

of desire's eternal return
with all its comforts and demands
to aging lovers and their querulous flesh?
The osculation of the sun:
the feel and look of light
falling on lovers and loved flesh
and smooth, tender, loved surfaces
and the whole loveless earth.

The osculation of the sun.
Why, it's an objective genitive—
and an objective generative, too!
I'm doing it again.
Words are doing it to me again.
Robert Kelly, have I you to thank
for all this heavy pack of syllables?

Osculation, occultation: why need we decide?
It is plain there is a polarity,
each requiring the other,
and now I see that it is
the sun's love and sweet sensuality
that brings him out of hiding,
out of that occlusion, that occultation,
out of that darkness where grains sprout,
the darkness that falls like an endless crucifixion
as each night we send the saviour
back to where he came from,
where he will not stay, returning
like a sacred lover with a kiss of light
that falls on this dusty and desirous world,
on the uplifted lips and thighs of maidens,
on the sprouting grain
leaping from the buried light of winter
to receive the holy kiss:
that lifts us clean out of metaphor,
into the endless light.

Etching

From six scraps of copper
trimmed from other plates
Lynn has created a landscape
shining under the moon.
From the waste of intended schemes
she has arranged a world,
carved with the stylus
and cut by etcher's acid
until the metal's secrets ·
are shining with old light.
And in this world are mountains
covered with forests
that look like memory,
and fabulous caves like mouths
of darkness in the moonlight;
and from the caves come animals,
eyes shining with the light
of undreamed, forgotten zodiacs,
and they speak of the waters
flowing under the earth
and of the unknown beings
in light and water and air and metals
and of all the secrets lying
hidden in the ores of the earth,
in seams of lead and silver
leading down into the depths:
and all these things lie potent
and hidden in six scraps of copper
and some wasted schemes;
images are flying forth
like sacred bats stitching
through the riches of the night.
How many other things lie
waiting to be discovered
where I have never thought to look?